Ages 5 and Up

Alfred's

Kid's Piano Course 1

The Easiest Piano Method Ever!

Christine H. Barden • Gayle Kowalchyk • E. L. Lancaster

Alfred

Alfred Music
P.O. Box 10003
Van Nuys, CA 91410-0003
alfred.com

Copyright © MMX, MMXVI by Alfred Music
All rights reserved. Printed in USA.

ISBN-10: 1-4706-3351-5 (Book & Online Audio)
ISBN-13: 978-1-4706-3351-6 (Book & Online Audio)
ISBN-10: 1-4706-3352-3 (Book & DVD & Online Video/Audio)
ISBN-13: 978-1-4706-3352-3 (Book & DVD & Online Video/Audio)

Cover and interior illustrations by Jeff Shelly.

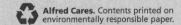 **Alfred Cares.** Contents printed on
environmentally responsible paper.

Contents

Included with this book are companion audio tracks that are available online to stream or download. An audio icon, like the one to the left, is beside the title of each example with an audio recording. The icon includes two track numbers: The first track number is for the student part alone, and the second track number is for the student part with colorful accompaniments. Follow the instructions on the inside front cover to access the audio tracks.

How to Sit at the Piano

To play well, it is important to sit correctly at the piano. Follow the instructions on this page so you are playing with good posture and hand position. You will also learn to sit at the correct height on the bench and at the right distance from the keyboard.

- Sit tall!
- Let your arms hang loosely from your shoulders.
- Place the bench facing the piano squarely.
- Keep your knees slightly under the keyboard.

If you are small:

- Sit on a book or cushion.

If your feet don't touch the floor:

- Place a book or stool under your feet.

Curve Your Fingers!

Always curve your fingers when you play.

1. Practice pretending to hold a bubble in your hand.
2. Shape your hand and hold the bubble gently, so that it doesn't pop.
3. Use this hand position on the keyboard.

Left-Hand Finger Numbers

Fingers are given numbers for playing the piano. The thumb is finger 1, and pinky is finger 5. Memorize the numbers of all your fingers.

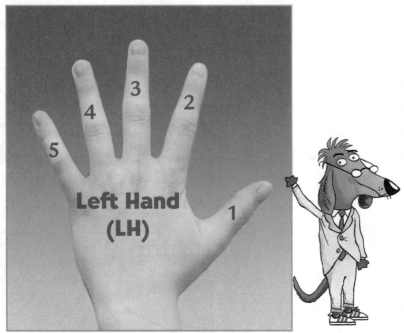

Hold up your **left hand** and wiggle each finger:

- Finger 1 (Thumbkin)
- Finger 2 (Pointer)
- Finger 3 (Tall Man)
- Finger 4 (Ring Man)
- Finger 5 (Pinky)

Activity

Draw an outline of your left hand in the space below and number each finger.

Right-Hand Finger Numbers

The fingers of the right hand are numbered the same way as the left hand. Put your hands together, with fingers touching, and steadily tap finger 1 of both hands against each other. Then tap together finger 2 of both hands, then finger 3, finger 4, and finger 5.

Hold up your **right hand** and wiggle each finger:

- Finger 1 (Thumbkin)
- Finger 2 (Pointer)
- Finger 3 (Tall Man)
- Finger 4 (Ring Man)
- Finger 5 (Pinky)

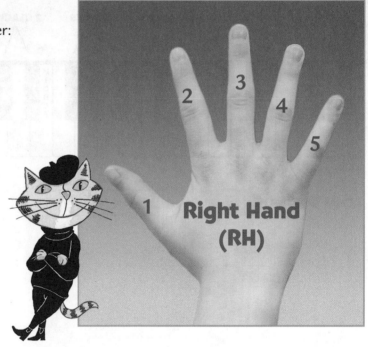

Activity

Draw an outline of your right hand in the space below and number each finger.

The Keyboard

The keyboard has white keys and black keys. The keys on the left side of the keyboard make low sounds. The keys on the right make high sounds.

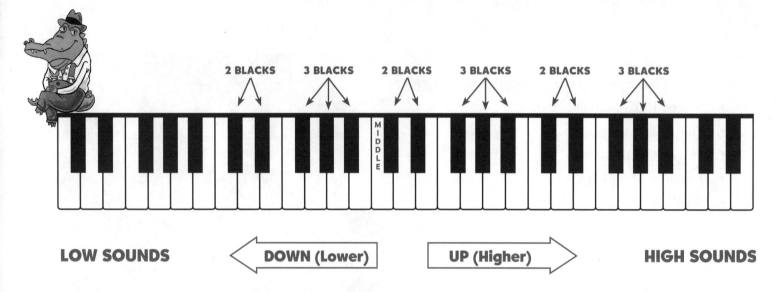

2 BLACKS   3 BLACKS   2 BLACKS   3 BLACKS   2 BLACKS   3 BLACKS

M
I
D
D
L
E

LOW SOUNDS   ← DOWN (Lower)   UP (Higher) →   HIGH SOUNDS

Two-Black-Key Groups

Two-black-key groups are easy to find. Count the number of two-black-key groups on your keyboard.

LH

3 2

Using LH fingers 2 and 3 together, begin at the middle of the keyboard and play both notes of each two-black-key group going down to the bottom of the keyboard.

Do the sounds get **higher** or **lower**?_____

RH

2 3

Using RH fingers 2 and 3 together, begin at the middle of the keyboard and play both notes of each two-black-key group going up to the top of the keyboard.

Do the sounds get **higher** or **lower**?_____

6

Three-Black-Key Groups

Three-black-key groups alternate with two-black-key groups. Count the number of three-black-key groups on your keyboard.

LH

Using LH fingers 2, 3, and 4 together, begin at the middle of the keyboard and play all three notes of each three-black-key group going down to the bottom of the keyboard.

Do the sounds get **higher** or **lower**?_____

RH

Using RH fingers 2, 3, and 4 together, begin at the middle of the keyboard and play all three notes of each three-black-key group going up to the top of the keyboard.

Do the sounds get **higher** or **lower**?_____

Activity

1. Circle each group of two black keys.

2. Draw a box around each group of three black keys.

Playing Two Black Keys

Symbols that show how loud or soft to play are called *dynamics*. These symbols come from Italian words.

Loud Sounds

f

The sign *f* stands for *forte*, which means to play **loud**.

Using LH fingers 2 and 3, play two black keys **low** on the keyboard at once. Play the two keys loudly (*f*) on each word as you say,

"I can play two low black keys."

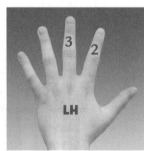

Soft Sounds

p

The sign *p* stands for *piano*, which means to play **soft**.

Using RH fingers 2 and 3, play two black keys **high** on the keyboard at once. Play the two keys softly (*p*) on each word as you say,

"I can play two high black keys."

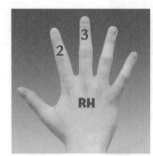

Using fingers 2 and 3 of either hand, play **all** the two-black-key groups on the entire keyboard.

Quarter Note

Introducing the Quarter Note

Each quarter note has a round black circle called a *notehead* with a line called a *stem*.

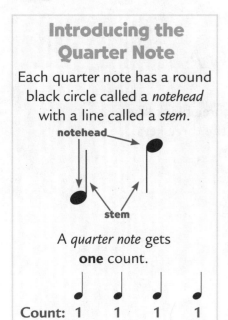

notehead

stem

A *quarter note* gets **one** count.

Count: 1   1   1   1

Bar lines divide the music into equal *measures*.

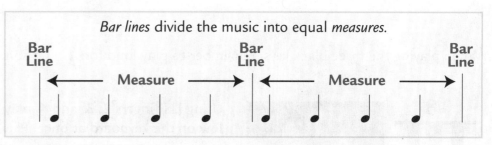

Bar Line

Bar Line

Bar Line

Measure

Measure

Practice Directions

Now it is time to play your first pieces on the keyboard. Follow these practice directions.

1. Point to the quarter notes in the songs below and count aloud evenly.
2. Play one key at a time and say the finger numbers.
3. Play and sing the words.

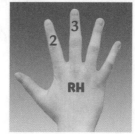

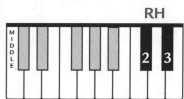

RH

Right-Hand Marching Track 1 (45)

DOUBLE BAR used at the end

f 2   3   2   3   2   3   2   3

Count: 1   1   1   1   1   1   1   1
Right hand march - ing   2   3   2   3

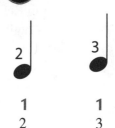

LH

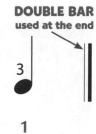

LH

Left-Hand Walking  Track 2 (46)

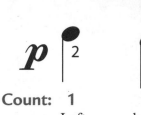

p 2   3   2   3   2   3   2   3

Count: 1   1   1   1   1   1   1   1
Left hand walk - ing,   2   3   2   3

9

Playing Three Black Keys

When playing the three black keys, remember to play loud for f and soft for p.

LH

 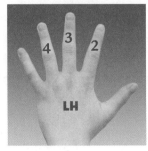

Using LH fingers 2, 3, and 4, play three black keys **low** on the keyboard at once. Play the three keys softly (p) on each word as you say,

"I can play three low black keys."

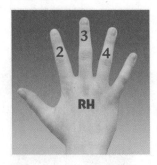 **RH**

Using RH fingers 2, 3, and 4, play three black keys **high** on the keyboard at once. Play the three keys loudly (f) on each word as you say,

"I can play three high black keys."

Using fingers 2, 3, and 4 of either hand, play **all** the three-black-key groups on the entire keyboard.

Quarter Rest

Introducing the Quarter Rest

Rests are signs of **silence**. They tell you to lift your hand to stop the sound.

A *quarter rest*

𝄾

gets **one** count.

Practice Directions

Follow the practice directions on page 9 as you play these pieces.

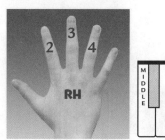

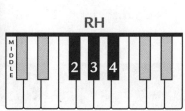

A Mouse's Melody   Track 3 (47)

RH

p

Count: 1   1   1 (Rest)   1   1   1 (Rest)   1   1   1 (Rest)

Lit - tle mouse   plays and then   runs a - way.

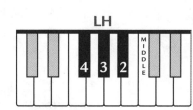

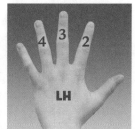

A Bear's Song   Track 4 (48)

LH

f

Count: 1   1   1 (Rest)   1   1   1 (Rest)   1   1   1 (Rest)

My bear's song   is not long.   Now it's gone.

Half Note

Introducing the Half Note

A *half note* gets **two** counts. It is twice as long as a quarter note.

Count: 1 – 2   1 – 2

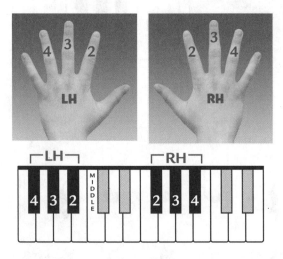

Practice Directions

Follow the practice directions on page 9 as you play "Hot Cross Buns."

The right hand plays the top line, and the left hand plays the bottom line.

Hot Cross Buns Track 5 (49)

RH

f

Count: 1   1   1 - 2   1   1   1 - 2   1   1   1   1   1   1   1 - 2

Hot cross buns!   Hot cross buns!   Yum - my, yum - my, hot cross buns!

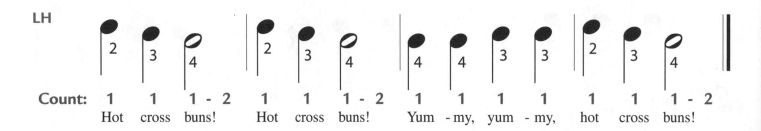

LH

Count: 1   1   1 - 2   1   1   1 - 2   1   1   1   1   1   1   1 - 2

Hot cross buns!   Hot cross buns!   Yum - my, yum - my, hot cross buns!

Whole Note

Introducing the Whole Note

o   Count: 1 – 2 – 3 – 4

A *whole note* gets **four** counts. It is as long as two half notes or four quarter notes.

Practice Directions

Follow the practice directions on page 9 as you play "Old MacDonald Had a Farm." The right hand alternates with the left hand on each line.

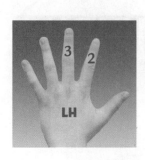
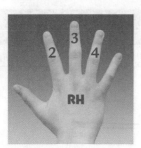

Old MacDonald Had a Farm  Track 6 (50)

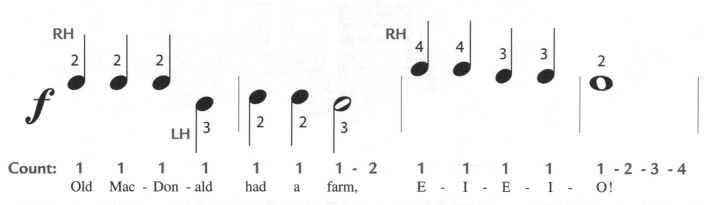

Count: 1 1 1 1 1 1 1-2 1 1 1 1 1-2-3-4
Old Mac-Don-ald had a farm, E - I - E - I - O!

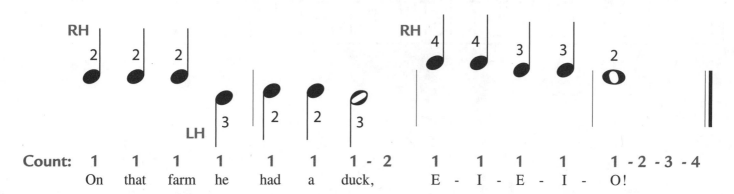

Count: 1 1 1 1 1 1 1-2 1 1 1 1 1-2-3-4
On that farm he had a duck, E - I - E - I - O!

13

White Keys

The white keys are named for the first seven letters of the alphabet:

A B C D E F G

The lowest key on the keyboard is A.

The highest key on the keyboard is C.

LOW   A B C D E F G A B C D E F G A B C D E F G A B C D E F G A B C D E F G A B C D E F G A B C D E F G A B C   HIGH

↑ Middle C

Did You Notice?
The key names are used over and over!

Write the name of each white key on the keyboard below.

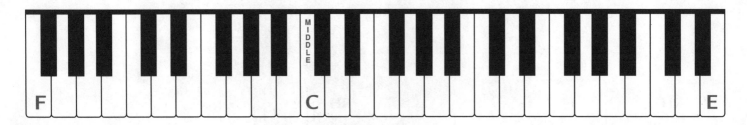

F   C   E

Finding D on the Keyboard

D is the white key in the middle of a two-black-key group.

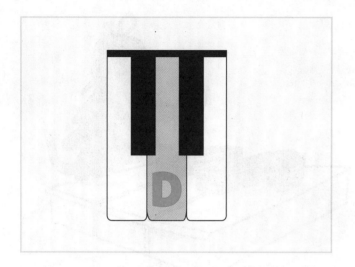

Find each D on the keyboard below and color it yellow.

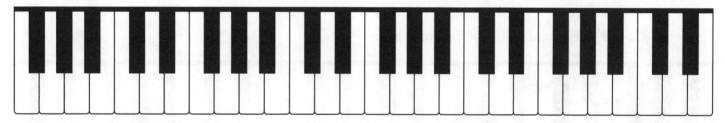

Practice Directions

1. Clap (or tap) and count aloud evenly.
2. Point to the notes and rests, and count aloud evenly.
3. Play and sing the words.

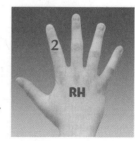

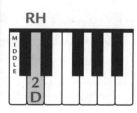

Use finger 2 (Pointer) to play each D in "The D Song."

The D Song Track 7 (51)

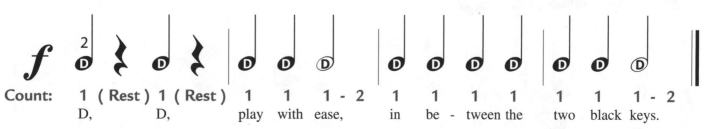

Count:	1	(Rest)	1	(Rest)	1	1	1 - 2	1	1	1	1	1	1	1 - 2
	D,		D,		play	with	ease,	in	be -	tween	the	two	black	keys.

15

Finding C on the Keyboard

C is the white key to the left of a two-black-key group.

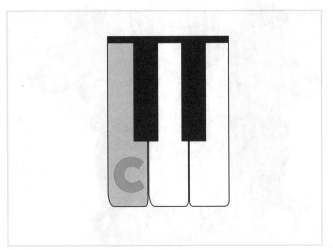

Find each C on the keyboard below and color it green.

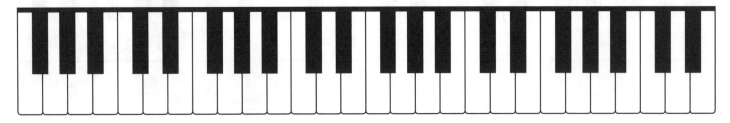

Practice Directions

Follow the practice directions on page 15 as you play "The C Song." Use finger 1 (Thumbkin) to play each C.

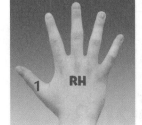

The C Song 🔊 Track 8 (52)

C,   C,   if   you   please,   just   be - low   the   two   black keys.

Finding E on the Keyboard

E is the white key to the right of a two-black-key group.

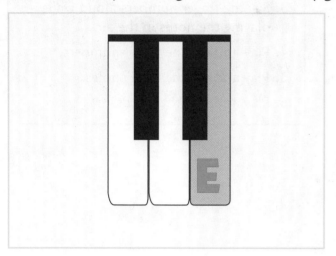

Find each E on the keyboard below and color it red.

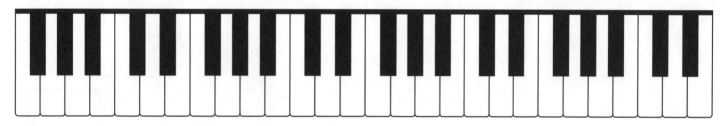

Practice Directions

Follow the practice directions on page 15 as you play "The E Song." Use finger 3 (Tall Man) to play each E.

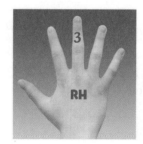

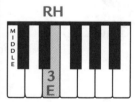

The E Song  Track 9 (53)

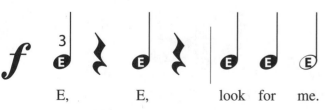

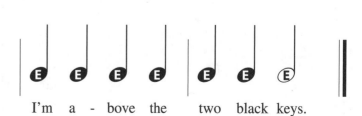

E,   E,   look for me.   I'm a - bove the   two black keys.

Practice Directions

1. Clap (or tap) and count aloud evenly.
2. Point to the notes and rests, and count aloud evenly.
3. Say the finger numbers aloud while playing the notes in the air.
4. Play and say the finger numbers.
5. Play and say the note names.
6. Play and sing the words.

"Go Tell Aunt Rhody" for right hand uses fingers 1, 2, and 3.

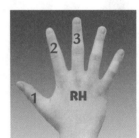
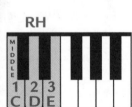

Go Tell Aunt Rhody (for RH)

Track 10 (54)

Count: 1 - 2   1   1   1 - 2   1 - 2   1 - 2   1   1   1   1   1 - 2
Go   tell   Aunt   Rho - dy,   go   tell   Aunt   Rho - dy,

Skip 2 on D

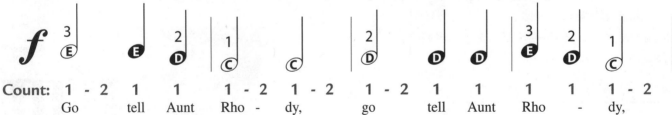

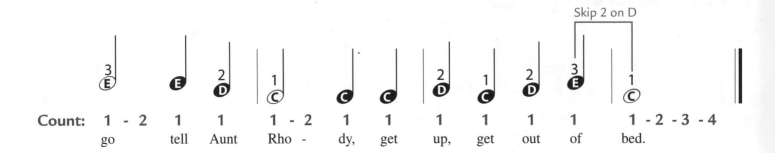

Count: 1 - 2   1   1   1 - 2   1   1   1   1   1   1   1 - 2 - 3 - 4
go   tell   Aunt   Rho - dy,   get   up,   get   out   of   bed.

Practice Directions

Follow the practice directions on page 18.

After you have learned to play "Go Tell Aunt Rhody" on both pages 18 and 19, play them without stopping in between to create a longer song.

"Go Tell Aunt Rhody" for left hand uses fingers 3 on C, 2 on D, and 1 on E.

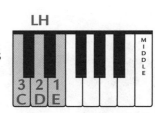

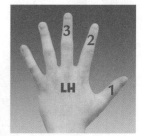

Go Tell Aunt Rhody (for LH) 🔊 Track 11 (55)

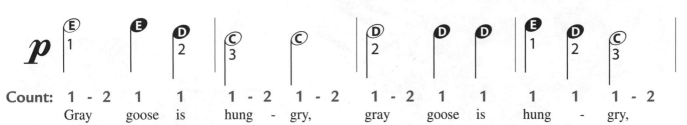

Count: 1 - 2 1 1 1 - 2 1 - 2 1 - 2 1 1 1 1 1 - 2

Gray goose is hung – gry, gray goose is hung – gry,

Skip 2 on D

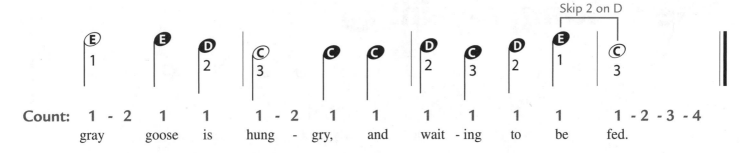

Count: 1 - 2 1 1 1 - 2 1 1 1 1 1 1 1 - 2 - 3 - 4

gray goose is hung – gry, and wait – ing to be fed.

Review: C, D, E

Draw a line from each key marked with an "X" in the first column to its note name in the second column.

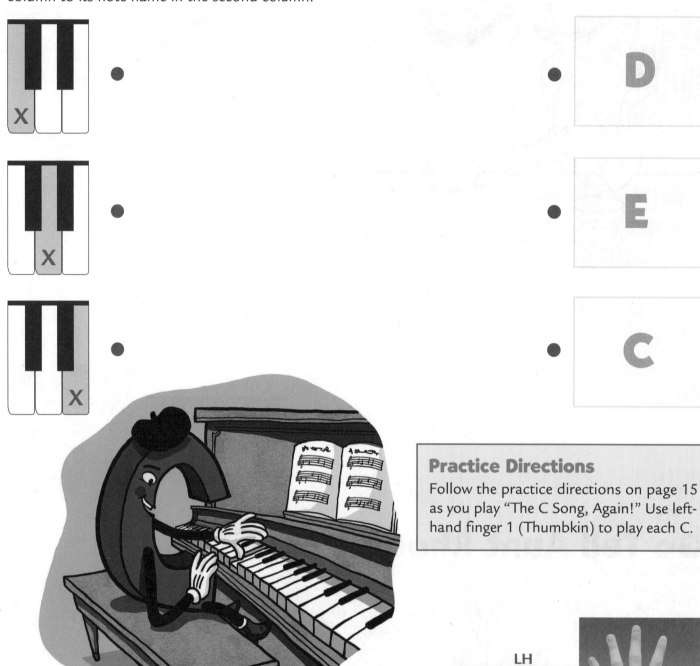

D

E

C

Practice Directions

Follow the practice directions on page 15 as you play "The C Song, Again!" Use left-hand finger 1 (Thumbkin) to play each C.

The C Song, Again! Track 12 (56)

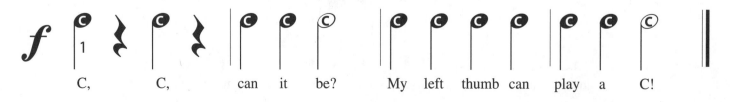

C,   C,   can it be?   My left thumb can play a C!

Finding B on the Keyboard

B is to the right of a three-black-key group.

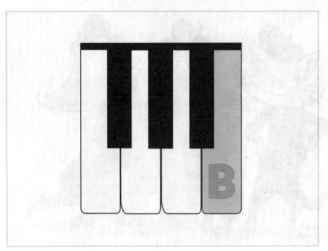

Find each B on the keyboard below and color it purple.

Practice Directions

Follow the practice directions on page 15 as you play "The B Song." Use left-hand finger 2 (Pointer) to play each B.

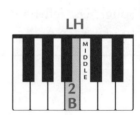

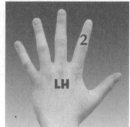

The B Song Track 13 (57)

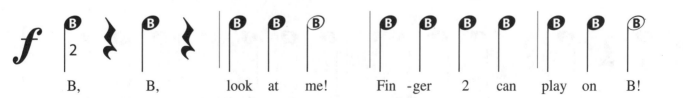

B,   B,   look   at   me!   Fin -ger   2   can   play   on   B!

Finding A on the Keyboard

A is the white key to the left of B.

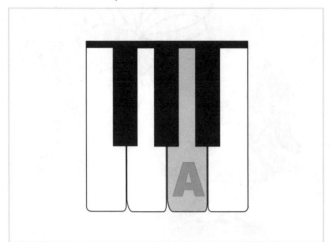

Find each A on the keyboard below and color it blue.

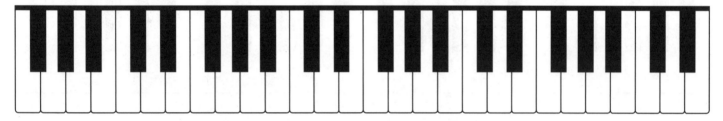

Practice Directions

Follow the practice directions on page 15 as you play "The A Song." Use left-hand finger 3 (Tall Man) to play each A.

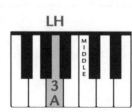

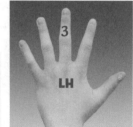

The A Song Track 14 (58)

A,   A,   hap - py day!   Fin - ger 3 can play on A!

Whole Rest

Introducing the Whole Rest

A *whole rest*
gets **four** counts. Rest for the
whole measure.

Count: Rest – 2 – 3 – 4

Practice Directions

Follow the practice directions on page 18
as you play "Little Dance" and "Rainy
Day." Remember to lift your hand for the
whole rests.

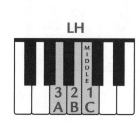

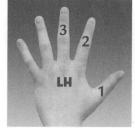

Little Dance  Track 15 (59)

Repeat Sign
Play again.

Count: 1   1   1 - 2   Rest - 2 - 3 - 4   1   1   1 - 2   Rest - 2 - 3 - 4
       Walk and stop.   Walk and stop.

Rainy Day Track 16 (60)

Count: 1   1   1   1   1   1   1   1   1   1   1   1   1 - 2 - 3 - 4
       Play -ing with my mus- ic friends on such a rain- y   day.

23

Finding F on the Keyboard

F is to the left of a three-black-key group.

Find each F on the keyboard below and color it pink.

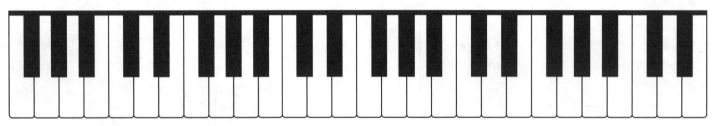

Practice Directions

Follow the practice directions on page 15 as you play "The F Song." Use right-hand finger 4 (Ring Man) to play each F.

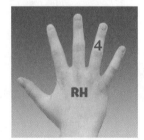

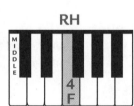

The F Song Track 17 (61)

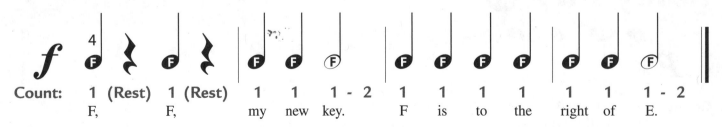

Count:	1	(Rest)	1	(Rest)	1	1	1 - 2	1	1	1	1	1	1	1 - 2
	F,		F,		my	new	key.	F	is	to	the	right	of	E.

Finding G on the Keyboard

G is the white key between F and A.

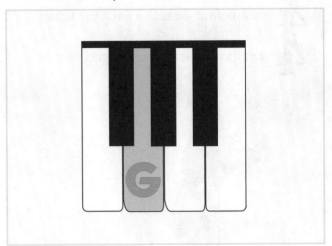

Find each G on the keyboard below and color it orange.

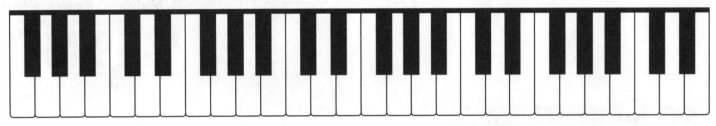

Practice Directions

Follow the practice directions on page 15 as you play "The G Song." Use right-hand finger 5 (Pinky) to play each G.

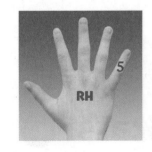

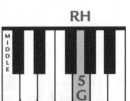

The G Song Track 18 (62)

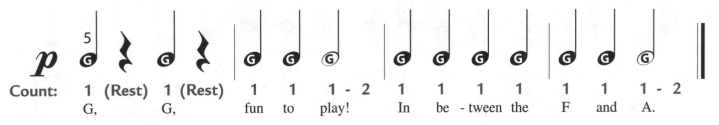

Count:	1	(Rest)	1	(Rest)	1	1	1 - 2	1	1	1	1	1	1	1 - 2
	G,		G,		fun	to	play!	In	be	- tween	the	F	and	A.

$\frac{4}{4}$ Time Signature

You know how many beats are in each measure by looking at the *time signature*, which is always at the beginning of the music.

$\frac{4}{4}$ means **four** beats to each measure.

$\frac{4}{4}$ means a **quarter note** ♩ gets one beat.

Practice Directions

Follow the practice directions on page 18 as you play "Ice Cream" and "Music Stars!"

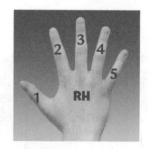

Middle C Position (RH)

Ice Cream  Track 19 (63)

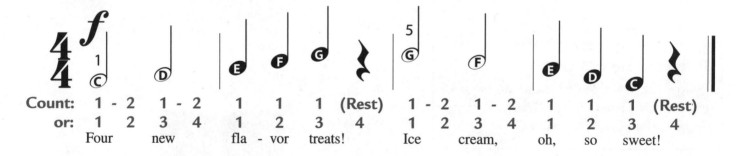

Count:	1 - 2	1 - 2	1	1	1 (Rest)	1 - 2	1 - 2	1	1	1 (Rest)
or:	1 2	3 4	1	2	3 4	1 2	3 4	1	2	3 4
	Four	new	fla - vor	treats!		Ice	cream,	oh,	so	sweet!	

Music Stars! Track 20 (64)

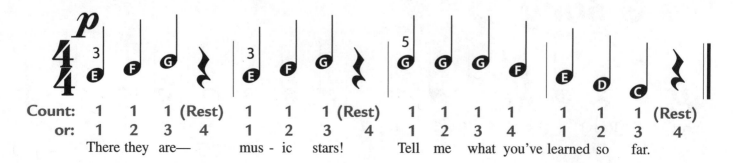

Count:	1	1	1 (Rest)	1	1	1 (Rest)	1	1	1	1	1	1	1 (Rest)
or:	1	2	3 4	1	2	3 4	1	2	3	4	1	2	3 4
	There	they	are—	mus -	ic	stars!	Tell	me	what	you've	learned	so	far.

3/4 Time & Dotted Half Notes

Introducing the Dotted Half Note

𝅗𝅥.

A *dotted half note* gets **three** counts. It looks like a half note with a dot to the right of the notehead.

𝅗𝅥.

Count: 1 - 2 - 3

3 means **three** beats to each measure.

4 means a **quarter note** ♩ gets one beat.

Practice Directions

Follow the practice directions on page 18 as you play the songs on this page.

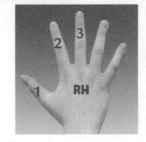

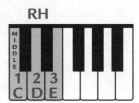

Ready to Play  Track 21 (65)

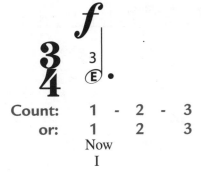

Count:	1 - 2 - 3	1 - 2 - 3	1	1	1	1 - 2 - 3
or:	1 2 3	1 2 3	1	2	3	1 2 3
	Now	it's	my	les	- son	day.
	I	am	read	- dy	to	play.

Middle C Position (LH)

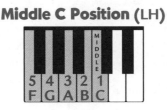

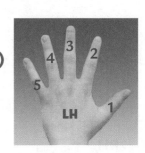

Play 3/4 Time  Track 22 (66)

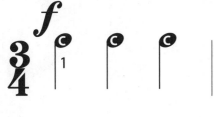

Count:	1	1	1	1	1	1	1	1	1	1 - 2 - 3
or:	1	2	3	1	2	3	1	2	3	1 2 3
	Three	beats	per	meas -	ure,	oh,	I'm	do -	ing	fine.
	It's	so	much	fun	when	I	play	3 -	4	time.

27

Moderately Loud Sounds

mf

The sign mf stands for
mezzo forte, which means to
play **moderately loud**.

Practice Directions
Follow the practice directions on page 18
as you play "Yankee Doodle."

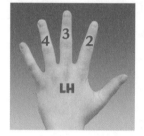
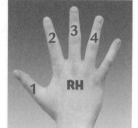
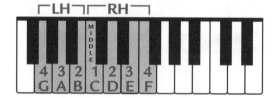

Yankee Doodle Track 23 (67)

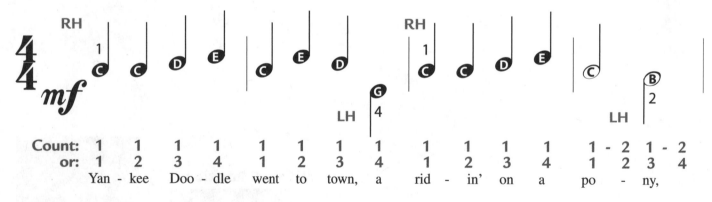

Count: 1   1   1   1   1   1   1   1   1   1   1   1   1 - 2 1 - 2
or: 1   2   3   4   1   2   3   4   1   2   3   4   1   2   3   4
Yan - kee Doo - dle went to town, a rid - in' on a po - ny,

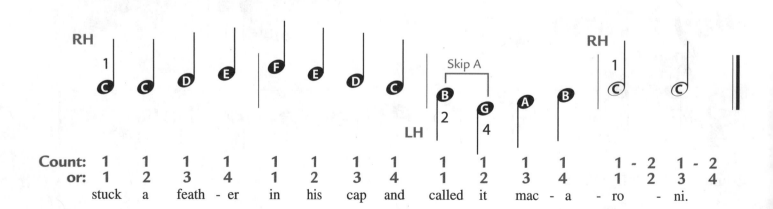

Count: 1   1   1   1   1   1   1   1   1   1   1   1   1 - 2 1 - 2
or: 1   2   3   4   1   2   3   4   1   2   3   4   1   2   3   4
stuck a feath - er in his cap and called it mac - a - ro - ni.

28

The Staff

Each note has a name. That name depends on where the note is found on the *staff*.
The staff is made up of five horizontal lines and the spaces between those lines.

Line Notes on the Staff

The staff has **five lines**.

Notes can be written **on** the lines.

Draw a red circle around each line note.

Space Notes on the Staff

The staff has **four spaces**.

Notes can be written **in** the spaces.

Draw a blue circle around each space note.

Treble Clef

As music notation progressed through history, the staff had 2 to 20 lines. Symbols were invented that would always give a reference point for all other notes. These symbols are called *clefs*.

Introducing the Treble Clef

Play *treble clef* notes with the right hand.

Treble Clef

Treble Clef Middle C

Middle C is the C nearest the middle of the piano keyboard.

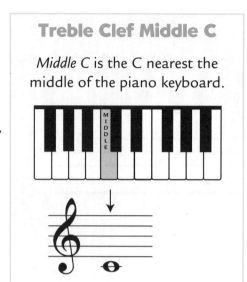

Trace the treble clef with a black crayon, and trace the middle C with a green crayon.

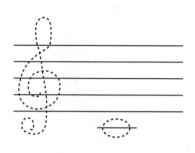

Steps

From one white key to the next, up or down, is a *step*.

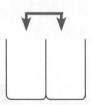

Steps are written **line to space** or **space to line**.

Treble Clef D

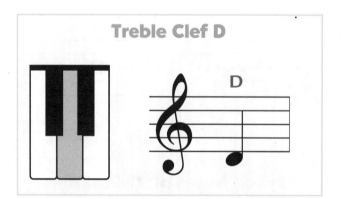

Practice Directions

Follow the practice directions on page 18 as you play "Take a Step." This song uses repeated notes and steps up and down.

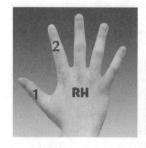

Take a Step Track 24 (68)

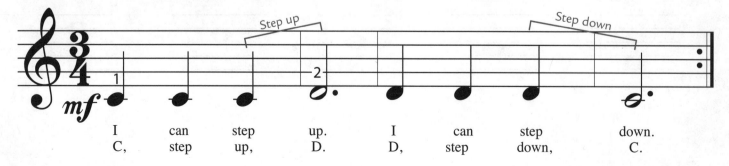

| | I | can | step | up. | I | can | step | down. |
| | C, | step | up, | D. | D, | step | down, | C. |

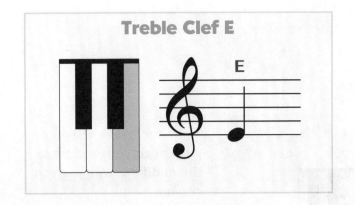

Treble Clef E

Practice Directions
Follow the practice directions on page 18 as you play the songs on this page.

Circle the repeated notes in "Stepping Fun."
All other notes are steps.

Stepping Fun  Track 25 (69)

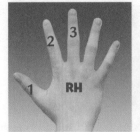
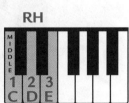

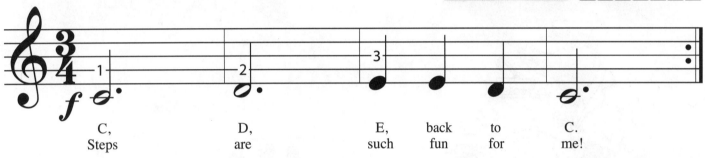

C,   D,   E,   back   to   C.
Steps   are   such   fun   for   me!

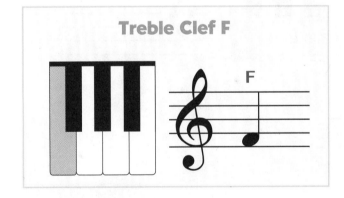

Treble Clef F

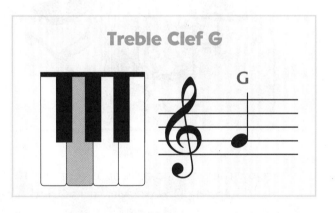

Treble Clef G

This song uses all five fingers of the right hand.

Right-Hand Song  Track 26 (70)

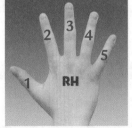
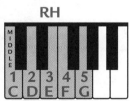

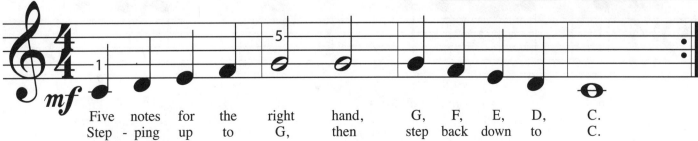

Five   notes   for   the   right   hand,   G,   F,   E,   D,   C.
Step - ping   up   to   G,   then   step   back   down   to   C.

31

Bass Clef

Introducing the Bass Clef

Play *bass clef* notes with the left hand.

Bass Clef

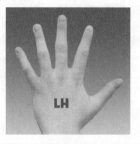

LH

Bass Clef Middle C

Trace the bass clef with a black crayon, and trace the middle C with a green crayon.

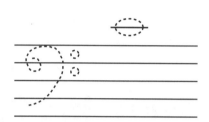

Bass Clef B

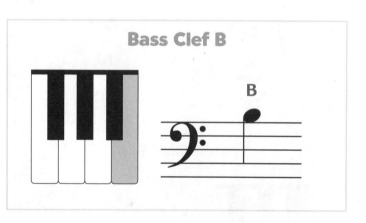

B

Practice Directions

Follow the practice directions on page 18 as you play "Stepping Down." Measures 2 and 4 of this song use repeated notes.

Stepping Down 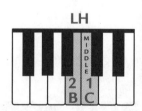 Track 27 (71)

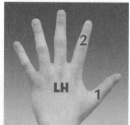

LH

2 B   1 C

mf

Step - ping down from mid - dle C,   C,   B,   look at me!
There's so much that I can do.   Step down, so can you.

32

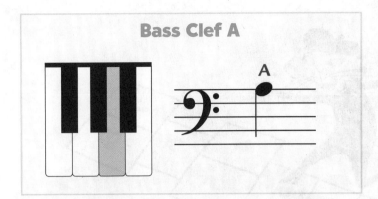

Bass Clef A

Practice Directions

Follow the practice directions on page 18 as you play the songs on this page.

Circle the repeated notes in "Music to Share." All other notes are steps.

Music to Share  Track 28 (72)

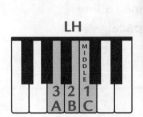
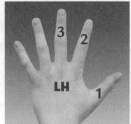

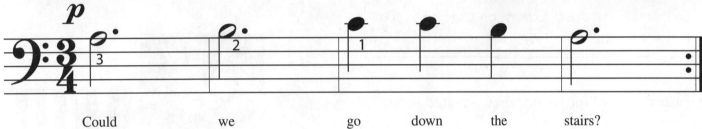

Could	we	go	down	the	stairs?
We	have	mu -	sic	to	share.

Bass Clef G

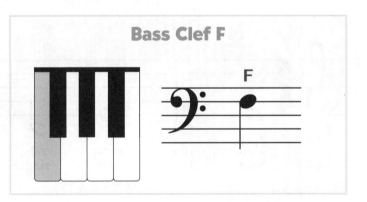

Bass Clef F

This song uses all five fingers of the left hand.

Left-Hand Song  Track 29 (73)

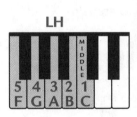
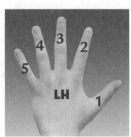

Five	notes	for	the	left	hand,	F,	G,	A,	B,	C.
Step	-ping	down	to	F,	then	step	back	up	to	C.

Skips

When you skip over a white key, you also skip a finger.

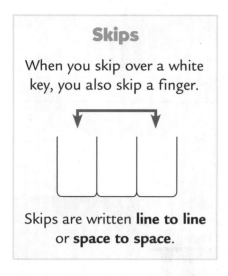

Skips are written **line to line** or **space to space**.

Practice Directions

Follow the practice directions on page 18 as you play the songs on this page.

Measure 3 of "Music Friend" uses repeated notes.

Music Friend 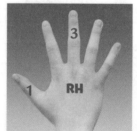 Track 30 (74)

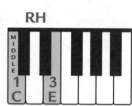

 Skip 2 on D

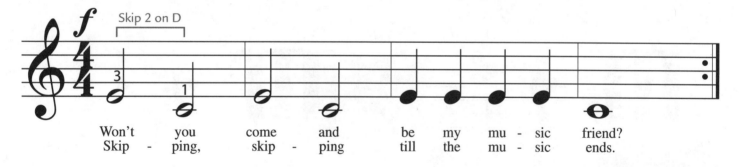

Won't   you   come   and   be   my   mu - sic   friend?
Skip - ping,   come   skip - ping   till   the   mu - sic   ends.

Find and circle the two steps in "Circle Time."

Circle Time Track 31 (75)

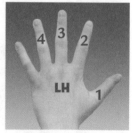

Skip 3 on A   Skip 2 on B

Cir - cling skips can   sure   be   fun!   In   this   piece there's   more than   one.
Grab   a   cray - on,   skip   to   B.   Find - ing   skips   is   fun   for   me!

The Grand Staff

When the treble staff and bass staff are joined together with a *brace*, it is called the *grand staff*. The grand staff is used to show notes for both the right and left hands.

A short line between the two staffs is used for **middle C**.

Brace

Middle C Position on the Grand Staff

When playing in middle C position, either thumb can play middle C.

Both hands of "Just for You" play steps, skips, and repeated notes.

Practice Directions
Follow the practice directions on page 18 as you play "Just for You."

Just for You  Track 32 (76)

Middle C Position
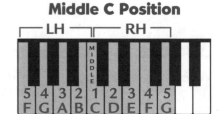

Hear the mu - sic I wrote just for you.

Now you know I think you're spe - cial, too!

Half Rest

Introducing the Half Rest

A *half rest* gets **two** counts. Do not play for two counts, which is the same as two quarter notes.

Count: Rest - 2
Or: 1   2

Practice Directions

Follow the practice directions on page 18 as you play "Haydn's Symphony."

Haydn's Symphony 🔊 Track 33 (77)

Middle C Position

Franz Joseph Haydn

mf Hay - dn wrote a sym - pho - ny. I will play it beau - ti - f'ly.

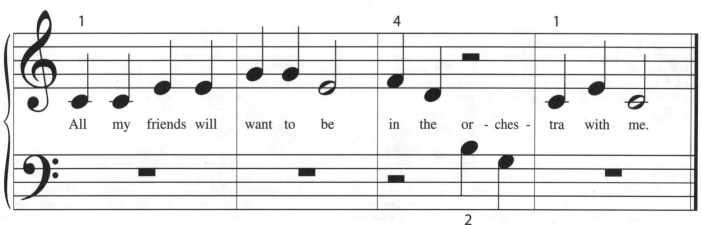

All my friends will want to be in the or - ches - tra with me.

London Bridge  Track 34 (78)

Middle C Position

Notice that both hands begin with finger 2 for this song.

Practice Directions
See page 18.

Lon - don Bridge is fall - ing down, fall - ing down, fall - ing down.

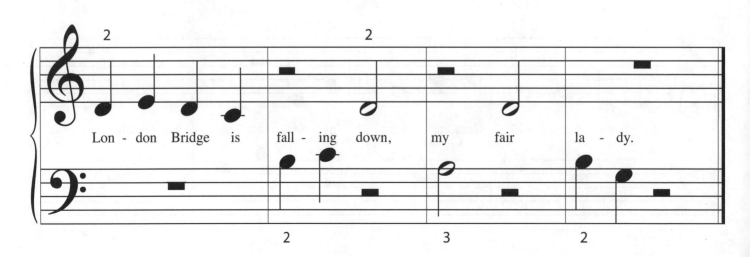

Lon - don Bridge is fall - ing down, my fair la - dy.

38

Twinkle, Twinkle, Little Star

Middle C Position

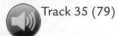
Track 35 (79)

mf Twin - kle, twin - kle, lit - tle star, how I won - der what you are!

Up a - bove the world so high, like a dia - mond in the sky,

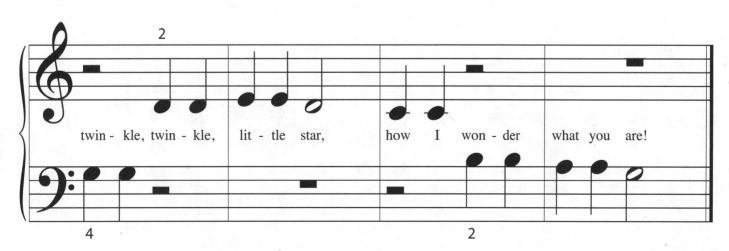

twin - kle, twin - kle, lit - tle star, how I won - der what you are!

Jingle Bells

Middle C Position

Track 36 (80)

James S. Pierpont

Jin - gle bells! Jin - gle bells! Jin - gle all the way!

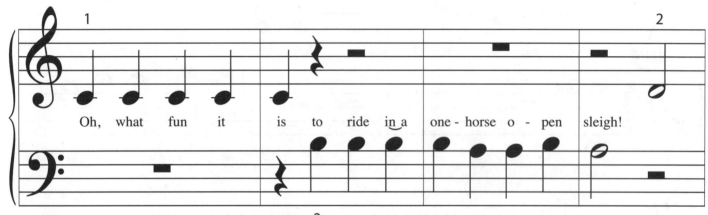

Oh, what fun it is to ride in a one-horse o - pen sleigh!

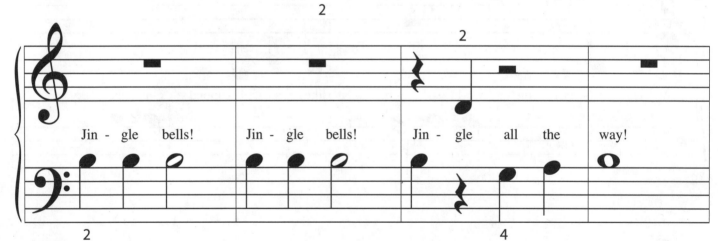

Jin - gle bells! Jin - gle bells! Jin - gle all the way!

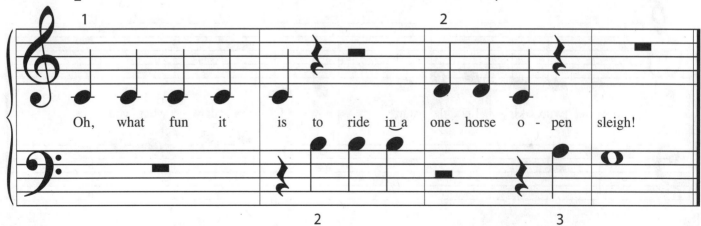

Oh, what fun it is to ride in a one-horse o - pen sleigh!

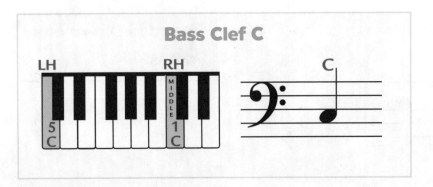

Bass Clef C

Practice Directions
See page 18.

New C 🔊 Track 37 (81)

Both hands play C.

Start on — / Mid - dle — / Mid - dle C, / C I know. / switch to Bass C / This new C is / 1 - 2 - 3. / down be - low.

Bass Clef D

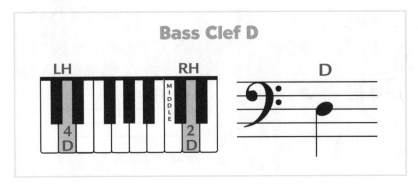

Three "D"-lightful Friends 🔊 Track 38 (82)

Both hands play D.

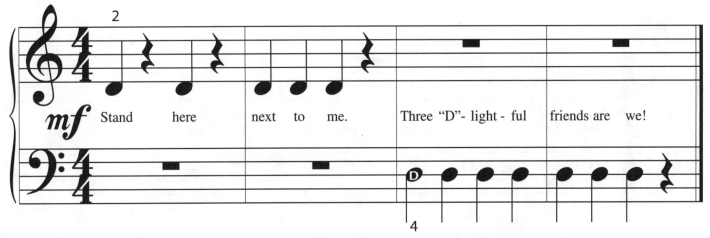

Stand here / next to me. / Three "D"- light - ful / friends are we!

41

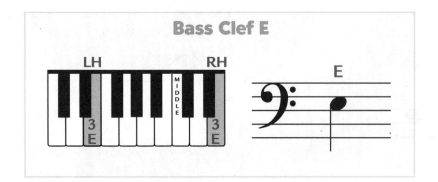

Bass Clef E

Practice Directions
See page 18.

Finger 3 on E 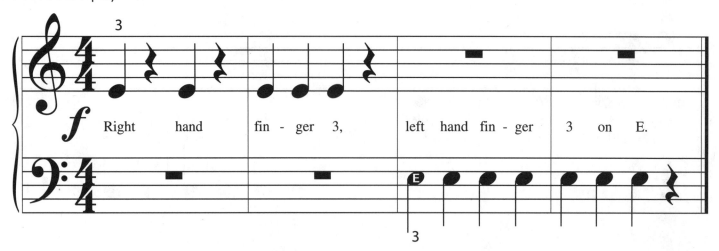 Track 39 (83)

Both hands play E.

Right hand fin - ger 3, left hand fin - ger 3 on E.

F in C Position

G in C Position

Great Big Day Track 40 (84)

C Position

This song uses all five fingers of the left hand.

C Position for LH

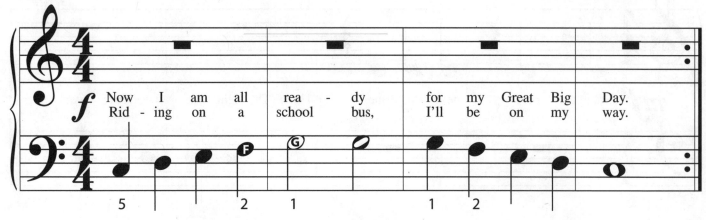

Now I am all rea - dy for my Great Big Day.
Rid - ing on a school bus, I'll be on my way.

42

C Position on the Grand Staff

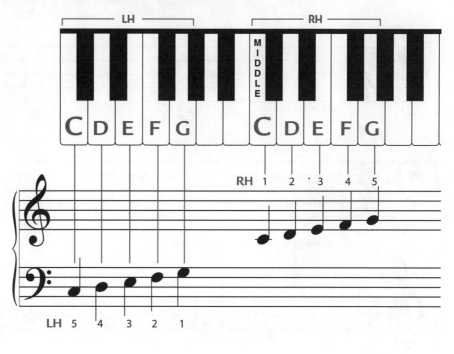

Ode to Joy 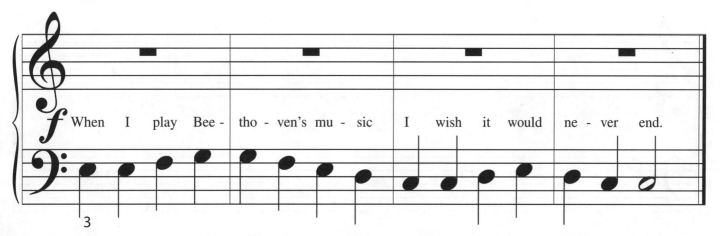 Track 41 (85)

(Theme from the Ninth Symphony)

Both hands begin with finger 3 on E.

Ludwig van Beethoven

Practice Directions
See page 18.

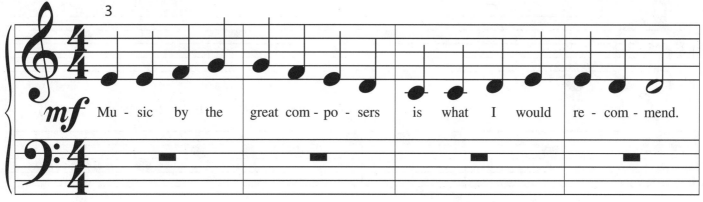

mf Mu - sic by the great com - po - sers is what I would re - com - mend.

f When I play Bee - tho - ven's mu - sic I wish it would ne - ver end.

Row, Row, Row Your Boat

C Position

Track 42 (86)

Practice Directions
See page 18.

A whole rest gets three beats in ¾ time.

Row, row, row your boat,

gent - ly down the stream.

Mer - ri - ly, mer - ri - ly, mer - ri - ly, mer - ri - ly,

life is but a dream.

Hush, Little Baby

C Position

 Track 43 (87)

Practice Directions
See page 18.

Each line begins with the left hand
and then changes to the right.

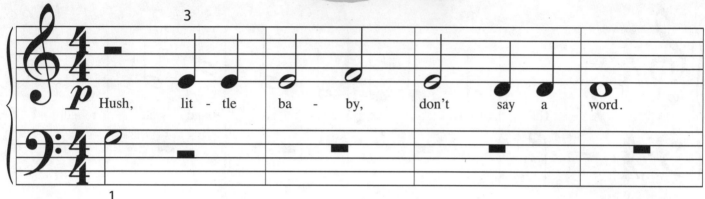

Hush,   lit - tle   ba - by,   don't   say   a   word.

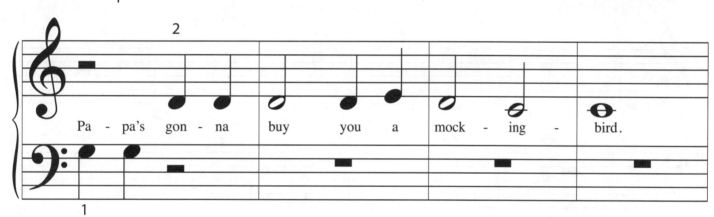

Pa - pa's   gon - na   buy   you   a   mock - ing - bird.

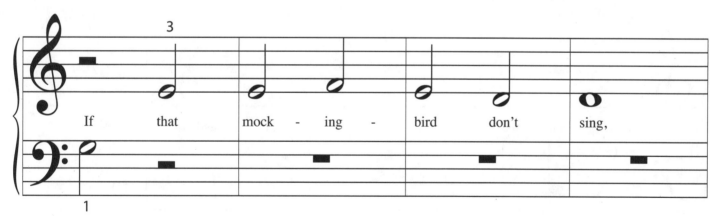

If   that   mock - ing - bird   don't   sing,

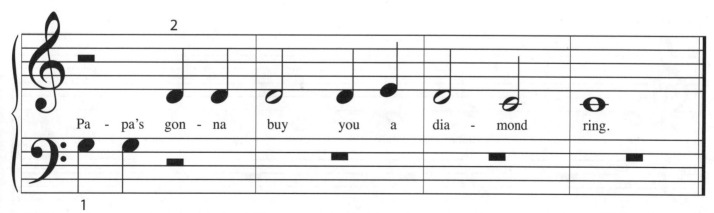

Pa - pa's   gon - na   buy   you   a   dia - mond   ring.

The Wheels on the Bus Track 44 (88)

C Position

Practice Directions
See page 18.

The wheels on the bus go round and round,

round and round, round and round. The

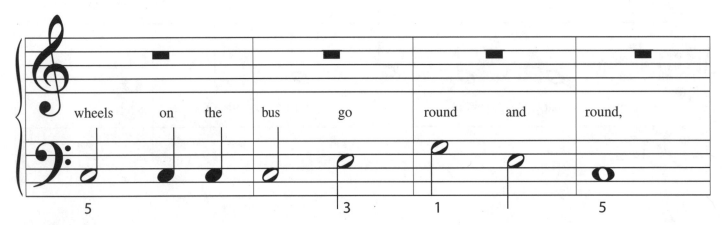

wheels on the bus go round and round,

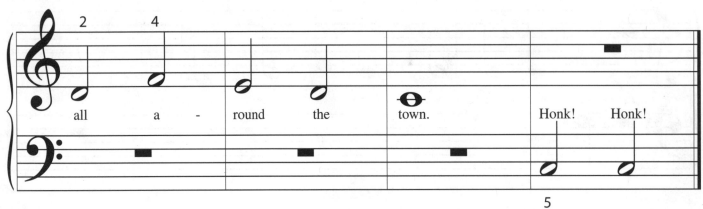

all a - round the town. Honk! Honk!

46

Music Matching Games

Symbols

Draw a line to match each symbol on the left to its name on the right.

1. ♩
2. ¾
3. ːǀǀ
4. *mf*
5. ▬
6. 𝅝
7. ˆ
8. *f*
9. ♩
10. *p*
11. ⁴⁄₄
12. ▬
13. ♩·

repeat sign

moderately loud

three beats in each measure

quarter rest

quarter note

loud

four beats in each measure

dotted half note

whole note

half rest

half note

whole rest

soft

Treble Clef Notes

Draw a line to match each treble clef note on the left to its correct letter name on the right.

1.

2.

3.

4.

5.

C

D

E

F

G

Bass Clef Notes

Draw a line to match each bass clef note on the left to its correct letter name on the right.

1.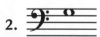
2.
3.
4.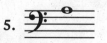
5.
6.
7.

C

D

E

F

G

A

B

Answer Key

Treble Clef Notes
1. G
2. D
3. C
4. E
5. F

Bass Clef Notes
1. D
2. G
3. C
4. B
5. A
6. F
7. E

Symbols
1. quarter note
2. three beats in each measure
3. repeat sign
4. moderately loud
5. half rest
6. whole note
7. quarter rest
8. loud
9. half note
10. soft
11. four beats in each measure
12. whole rest
13. dotted half note

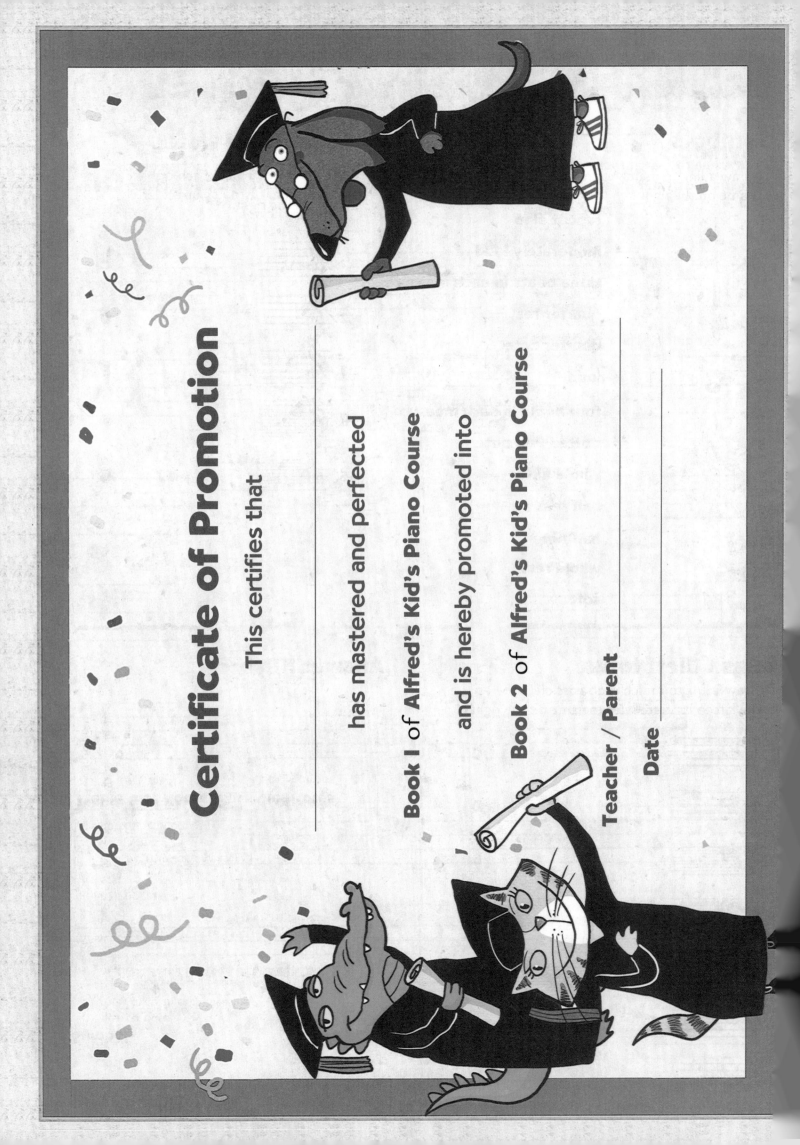

Certificate of Promotion

This certifies that

_____

has mastered and perfected

Book 1 of **Alfred's Kid's Piano Course**

and is hereby promoted into

Book 2 of **Alfred's Kid's Piano Course**

_____
Teacher / Parent

_____
Date